Table of Contents

INTRODUCTION

The allure of financial freedom whispers promises of early retirement, dream vacations, and the ability to pursue passions without the constraints of a traditional 9-to-5. But achieving this coveted freedom often requires more than just relying on a single income stream. Enter the world of side hustles – a vibrant ecosystem where creativity meets opportunity, and where the pursuit of extra income transforms into a journey of personal and financial growth.

This eBook serves as your compass, guiding you through a labyrinth of 20 diverse and exciting side hustle ideas. Whether you're a seasoned professional seeking a creative outlet, a student looking to supplement their income, or simply someone yearning for greater financial security, these ideas offer a pathway to unlock your earning potential and achieve your financial aspirations.

We'll delve into the realm of online freelancing, explore the potential of local service businesses, and uncover hidden gems in the world of creative entrepreneurship. You'll learn how to identify your unique skills and passions, transform them into profitable ventures, and build a sustainable side hustle that aligns with your lifestyle and goals.

But this eBook is more than just a list of ideas; it's a roadmap for success. We'll equip you with the knowledge and tools you need to launch your side hustle with confidence. From creating a solid business plan and developing effective marketing strategies to navigating the legal and financial aspects of self-employment, we'll cover all the essential steps to turn your side hustle dreams into a reality.

So, whether you're a seasoned entrepreneur or just starting your journey, let this ebook be your guide. Embrace the spirit of innovation, unleash your entrepreneurial potential, and discover the freedom that comes with building multiple income streams. The path to financial freedom begins now.

Chapter 1: Online Side Hustles

The internet has revolutionized the way we work, and online side hustles are an excellent opportunity for individuals to earn income while leveraging their skills. Whether you're looking to work from home, set your own schedule, or tap into a global market, online freelancing offers numerous possibilities. Below are some of the most popular online side hustle categories.

1. Freelancing:

Freelancing allows individuals to work independently for various clients, offering their expertise on a project-by-project basis. Unlike traditional jobs, freelancers have the flexibility to choose their clients, hours, and rates. Platforms such as Upwork, Fiverr, and Freelancer.com are great places to find freelance gigs.

1.1 Writing

Writing is one of the most versatile and sought-after freelance services online. It covers a wide range of niches and formats, including:

Content Writing:
Content writers create informative and engaging articles, blog posts, and web content aimed at educating or entertaining readers. This can involve writing for various industries such as technology, health, travel, finance, and lifestyle. A strong command of the language and the ability to write in a compelling, reader-friendly manner is essential.

Copywriting:
Copywriting involves writing persuasive texts designed to drive action, such as ads, product descriptions, and email campaigns. Copywriters need to understand consumer psychology and be able to write catchy, convincing content that prompts readers to take specific actions, such as purchasing a product or signing up for a newsletter.

Editing and Proofreading:
Editors and proofreaders help polish written content to ensure it's clear, concise, and free of errors. While editing may involve improving structure, flow, and tone, proofreading focuses mainly on spelling, grammar, punctuation, and formatting mistakes. It requires keen attention to detail and an excellent understanding of language rules.

1.2 Graphic Design

Graphic design is a highly creative freelance field that focuses on creating visual content. From logos and branding to infographics and website design, graphic designers help businesses communicate visually with their audiences.

Graphic designers use tools like Adobe Photoshop, Illustrator, and Canva to create visually appealing graphics. Freelancers in this field must possess artistic skills, an understanding of design principles, and a solid grasp of client needs to produce effective designs.

1.3 Virtual Assistance

Virtual assistants (VAs) offer administrative support to businesses or individuals remotely. Tasks can range from managing emails and scheduling appointments to organizing files, making travel arrangements, and handling customer service inquiries. A virtual assistant needs excellent organizational and communication skills.

Many VAs work with entrepreneurs, small business owners, and busy executives, helping them save time and stay organized. Specialized VAs may handle social media management, content creation, or technical tasks, allowing them to offer more value to clients and charge higher rates.

1.4 Social Media Management

Social media managers handle the social presence of brands, businesses, or individuals. This includes content creation, posting, community engagement, and analyzing performance metrics. With nearly every business needing a strong online presence, social media management has become a high-demand skill.

Social media managers should be well-versed in platforms like Facebook, Instagram, Twitter, LinkedIn, and TikTok. Creativity, attention to detail, and the ability to adapt to trends are essential skills for success in this field.

1.5 Web Development

Web development is the process of building websites, and it requires knowledge of programming languages like HTML, CSS, JavaScript, and frameworks such as React or WordPress. Web developers are responsible for both the technical functionality and user experience (UX) of a site.

This field offers lucrative opportunities, especially for developers with expertise in niche areas such as e-commerce platforms, mobile app development, or custom websites. Many clients look for web developers to build or maintain their sites, offering long-term work or higher-paying contracts.

1.6 Transcription

Transcription involves converting audio or video content into written text. This work requires strong listening and typing skills. Freelance transcriptionists can transcribe podcasts, interviews, webinars, meetings, and even court proceedings.

There are specialized areas within transcription, such as medical or legal transcription, which often require additional knowledge or certifications but tend to pay better. Accuracy and speed are critical in transcription work, and clients often seek those who can deliver high-quality, error-free content.

Types of Transcription:

- **Verbatim Transcription:** This is the most common type, where every word spoken in the recording is transcribed exactly as it is heard, including pauses, stutters, and filler words.
- **Non-Verbatim Transcription:** This type involves editing the transcribed text to improve clarity and readability. It may involve removing unnecessary words, correcting grammatical errors, and summarizing key points.
- **Specialized Transcription:** This type caters to specific industries or purposes, such as legal, medical, or educational settings. It may require specialized knowledge or formatting

Transcription Methods:

- **Manual Transcription:** This involves a human transcriber listening to the recording and typing out the text. It is a time-consuming process but ensures high accuracy.
- **Automated Transcription:** This uses speech recognition software to convert audio to text. It is faster but may require human review to correct errors.

Transcription Tools and Software:

- **Transcription Software:** Dragon NaturallySpeaking, Express Scribe, Transcribe
- **Online Transcription Services:** Rev, Temi, Otter.ai
- **Transcription Editors:** Audacity, Adobe Audition

Transcription Tips:

- **Use headphones:** This helps to isolate the audio and reduce background noise.
- **Take breaks:** Transcription can be mentally taxing, so it's important to take breaks to avoid

20 Untapped Income Streams 2025   By Wasike Cornelius

1.7 Translation

Translation services are in high demand, particularly for businesses or individuals looking to expand into international markets. Translators convert written content from one language to another, ensuring the meaning and context remain intact.

Successful translators must be fluent in at least two languages and understand cultural nuances. There is a significant market for specialized translation services, such as technical, legal, and medical translation, which can command higher rates. Platforms like Gengo and ProZ are popular for finding translation work.

1.8 Data Entry

Data entry involves inputting, updating, or organizing data in digital formats, often into spreadsheets or databases. The work can include tasks such as entering contact information, managing inventories, or updating records.

While the work may seem repetitive, it's ideal for individuals who are highly organized and can maintain a high level of accuracy. Data entry can be a great entry-level online side hustle, but experienced professionals who specialize in database management or big data analysis can earn more.

1.9 Online Tutoring

Online tutoring has surged in popularity, particularly in subjects such as mathematics, science, languages, and test preparation. Tutors assist students remotely, offering personalized teaching sessions via video conferencing platforms like Zoom.

The advantage of online tutoring is the flexibility to teach from anywhere and to set your own rates. Tutors with expertise in specialized fields or certifications (such as TEFL for English teaching) can command higher fees. Furthermore, platforms like VIPKid and Tutor.com provide an excellent entry point for new tutors.

Notes: Online side hustles have made it possible for anyone with a skill or passion to earn money from the comfort of their home. Freelancing offers flexibility and a diverse range of opportunities across various fields, from writing and design to tech and virtual assistance. By choosing a niche that aligns with your expertise, you can create a sustainable income stream while gaining experience and expanding your network.

2. Online Marketplaces

Online marketplaces connect sellers and buyers from around the world. These platforms are ideal for individuals who want to sell products, offer services, or monetize their expertise. Below are some of the most popular options:

2.1 Selling on Etsy

Etsy is a marketplace primarily focused on handmade crafts, vintage items, and digital products. Sellers can create custom items, such as jewelry, artwork, and home decor, or sell downloadable products like templates, planners, or pintables.

To succeed on Etsy:

- Focus on high-quality product photography to attract buyers.
- Write compelling product descriptions optimized for SEO.
- Engage with customers by offering excellent service and customization options.

Many sellers start Etsy stores as a side hustle and eventually grow them into full-fledged businesses.

2.2 Fiverr

Fiverr is a platform where freelancers offer services in a variety of categories, such as writing, graphic design, marketing, and tech. Services are called "gigs" and can start at $5, though experienced freelancers often charge significantly more.

Tips for thriving on Fiverr:

- Offer niche services that differentiate you from competitors.
- Build a strong profile with clear gig descriptions and a professional portfolio.
- Deliver high-quality work to earn positive reviews and attract more clients.

Fiverr is ideal for freelancers looking to start small and gradually build their reputation.

2.3 Upwork

Upwork is one of the largest platforms for freelancers to find projects. Unlike Fiverr, where clients choose gigs, Upwork allows freelancers to bid on job postings in various categories, such as writing, programming, and consulting.

To excel on Upwork:

- Create a polished profile showcasing your skills and experience.
- Apply to projects with personalized, thoughtful proposals.
- Focus on building a strong client base by delivering exceptional work and earning positive feedback.

Upwork is perfect for professionals who want to establish long-term relationships with clients and earn higher-paying contracts.

3. Content Creation

Content creation is a rewarding way to share your passions, build an audience, and monetize your expertise. While it often requires consistency and patience, successful content creators can generate significant income from multiple streams.

3.1 Blogging

Blogging involves creating written content on specific topics, such as travel, health, finance, or personal development. Bloggers earn money through ads, sponsored content, affiliate marketing, or selling their products.

Key tips for successful blogging:

- Choose a niche you're passionate about and knowledgeable in.
- Create high-quality, SEO-optimized content to attract readers.
- Monetize your blog by partnering with brands or using platforms like Google AdSense.

Blogging can start as a side hustle and eventually become a full-time income stream with consistent effort.

3.2 Vlogging

Vlogging is the video equivalent of blogging, where creators share their lives, interests, or expertise through platforms like YouTube. Popular vlogging niches include lifestyle, travel, tech reviews, and fitness.

To succeed in vlogging:

- Invest in good-quality equipment for filming and editing.
- Develop engaging, authentic content that resonates with your audience.
- Monetize through YouTube ads, sponsorships, or merchandise sales.

Vlogging can be a fun and creative way to earn money while connecting with viewers worldwide.

3.3 Podcasting

Podcasting involves creating audio content on specific topics or themes. Podcasts can cover anything from storytelling and interviews to education and entertainment.

How to thrive in podcasting:

- Select a compelling niche and develop a unique perspective or format.
- Use high-quality microphones and editing software for professional sound.
- Monetize through sponsorships, listener donations, or subscription services.

With the rising popularity of audio content, podcasting offers tremendous opportunities to build a loyal audience and earn a steady income.

3.4 Creating Online Courses

Online courses are a profitable way to share your expertise with others. Platforms like Udemy, Teachable, and Coursera allow you to create and sell courses on various topics, from coding to cooking.

Steps to create a successful online course:

- Identify a topic with high demand and market potential.
- Break down the content into clear, actionable lessons.
- Market your course effectively through social media, email newsletters, and partnerships.

Creating a course requires an upfront time investment, but it can generate passive income once it's live.

3.5 Selling Stock Photos and Videos

If you're skilled in photography or videography, selling stock content can be a great way to earn passive income. Platforms like Shutterstock, Adobe Stock, and Getty Images allow creators to upload and sell their photos and videos.

Tips for selling stock content:

- Focus on high-demand themes, such as business, travel, or lifestyle.
- Edit and tag your content effectively to increase visibility.
- Keep creating and uploading to build a diverse portfolio over time.

Stock content creators can earn royalties every time their work is downloaded, making it a scalable source of income.

Notes, Online marketplaces and content creation offer exciting opportunities for individuals to turn their skills, creativity, and passions into profitable ventures. Whether you're crafting handmade products, offering freelance services, or creating engaging content, the potential to earn and grow is virtually limitless. By choosing a path that aligns with your interests and investing the necessary time and effort, you can build a successful online side hustle and achieve financial freedom.

Chapter 2: Offline Side Hustles: Connecting with Your Community

The digital world offers a plethora of opportunities, but the heartbeat of a thriving side hustle often lies within the local community. These offline ventures offer a unique blend of personal interaction, community engagement, and the satisfaction of contributing directly to the needs of those around you.

2.1 Caring for Furry Friends: Pet Sitting and Dog Walking

For animal lovers, the joy of caring for pets can easily translate into a rewarding income stream. Pet sitting offers flexibility, allowing you to work around your own schedule while providing companionship and care for furry friends. Dog walking not only generates income but also encourages an active lifestyle and provides an opportunity to enjoy the outdoors.

Building a strong client base often starts with word-of-mouth referrals and leveraging local community platforms. Offering reliable and compassionate care is paramount. Going the extra mile – a quick playtime session in the park, a soothing massage, or even a thoughtful note for the owners – can solidify client relationships and foster long-term loyalty.

2.2 Home Sweet Home: House Sitting and Pet Sitting

When homeowners embark on vacations or business trips, they often seek trustworthy individuals to care for their homes and beloved pets. House sitting offers a unique opportunity to earn income while experiencing the comforts of a different environment.

Combining house sitting with pet sitting can significantly enhance your service offerings. This comprehensive package provides peace of mind to homeowners, knowing that their pets are receiving dedicated care while their home remains secure. Building trust is crucial in this line of work. Open communication, a respect for the homeowner's property, and a commitment to maintaining a clean and orderly environment are essential for long-term success.

2.3 Green Thumb Opportunities: Landscaping and Gardening

For those with a passion for plants and a love for the outdoors, landscaping and gardening offer fulfilling and rewarding side hustle options. The changing seasons bring a variety of opportunities – from spring cleanups and lawn mowing to fall leaf removal and winter garden preparations.

Expanding your service offerings beyond basic lawn care can increase your earning potential. Consider offering specialized services such as planting flowers and vegetable gardens, creating beautiful garden designs, and providing expert advice on plant care. Building a strong online presence through social media platforms and local community groups can help you connect with potential clients and showcase your expertise.

2.4 Running Errands and Lending a Hand: Personal Assistant Services

In today's fast-paced world, many individuals struggle to juggle the demands of work, family, and personal life. Offering personal assistant services can provide invaluable assistance to busy professionals and families.

Tailoring your services to meet individual needs is key. This could include grocery shopping, dry cleaning pick-up, appointment scheduling, bill payment, and even errand running. Building strong relationships with clients is crucial. Providing reliable, efficient, and personalized service while maintaining open communication will foster long-term client loyalty and referrals.

2.5 Spick and Span Solutions: Cleaning Services

Maintaining a clean and organized living or work environment is essential for both physical and mental well-being. Cleaning services are consistently in high demand, offering a steady stream of income for those who enjoy a hands-on approach.

Specializing in a particular niche can set you apart from the competition. Consider focusing on deep cleaning services, move-in/move-out cleaning, eco-friendly cleaning methods, or even specialized cleaning for businesses. Providing excellent customer service is paramount. Paying meticulous attention to detail, ensuring client satisfaction, and building a reputation for reliability and trustworthiness will ensure repeat business and positive referrals.

These are just a few examples of the many offline side hustle opportunities available within your local community. By identifying your skills, tapping into your passions, and providing exceptional service, you can transform these opportunities into thriving businesses while contributing to the well-being of those around you.

2.6. Food & Beverage Side Hustles

The food and beverage industry is a versatile field where innovation and quality can help you stand out. These side hustles are particularly suitable for those with culinary skills, a passion for food, or an entrepreneurial mindset.

Food and beverage side hustles, paired with creative ventures, offer unique and profitable ways to earn extra income while pursuing your passions. Whether you're delivering meals, crafting baked goods, or teaching art, these opportunities allow you to connect with your community, showcase your talents, and create a sustainable income stream. By focusing on quality, marketing effectively, and building relationships, you can turn these side hustles into thriving businesses.

The world of food and beverage offers a delectable array of side hustle opportunities, allowing individuals to share their culinary passions while generating income. From the convenience of food delivery to the excitement of a bustling food truck, these ventures cater to a diverse range of interests and skill levels.

Food delivery platforms like Uber Eats and DoorDash have transformed the way we dine, providing a flexible and accessible avenue for individuals seeking extra income. The allure of independent schedules and the potential for generous tips make this option particularly appealing. However, navigating the competitive landscape requires maintaining high delivery standards, ensuring prompt and courteous service, and cultivating a positive online reputation.

For those with a culinary flair and a touch of entrepreneurial spirit, the allure of a food truck or mobile food vendor is undeniable. The vibrant atmosphere of festivals, markets, and outdoor events provides a dynamic platform to showcase unique culinary creations. From gourmet burgers and artisanal tacos to handcrafted ice cream and delectable desserts, the possibilities are limited only by one's imagination. However, the initial investment in a food truck and the necessary equipment can be substantial. Furthermore, navigating local regulations and securing permits can require careful planning and attention to detail.

Catering services offer a more structured approach to the food and beverage industry, catering to a diverse clientele ranging from corporate events and weddings to intimate gatherings and social celebrations. Building a strong reputation for culinary excellence, impeccable service, and the ability to meet diverse dietary needs and preferences is paramount.

For those with a passion for baking and a knack for creating delicious treats, the world of bakesales and selling homemade goods offers a delightful avenue for entrepreneurial exploration. From delectable cakes and cookies to artisanal breads and decadent pastries, the possibilities are endless. However, adhering to food safety regulations, obtaining necessary permits, and effectively marketing your creations to the local community are crucial for success.

2.6.1 Food Delivery Services (Uber Eats, DoorDash)

Food delivery services are an excellent side hustle for individuals looking for flexibility and quick earnings. Platforms like Uber Eats, DoorDash, and Glovo allow you to deliver meals from local restaurants to customers in your area.

Advantages:

- Flexible hours that fit your schedule.
- Minimal upfront investment—usually a vehicle, bike, or scooter is enough to get started.
- Ability to work in high-demand areas for greater earnings.

Tips for Success:

- Choose peak hours (lunch and dinner) to maximize your income.
- Maintain good customer service to earn tips and high ratings.
- Optimize your delivery route to save time and fuel.

This side hustle is ideal for individuals who enjoy driving or cycling and want a steady flow of income.

2.6.2 Food Truck/Mobile Food Vendor

Operating a food truck or mobile food vending business allows you to take your culinary creations directly to customers. Popular options include selling street food, gourmet snacks, or beverages.

Advantages:

- Lower startup costs compared to opening a restaurant.
- Mobility allows you to target busy locations, events, or festivals.
- Opportunity to experiment with creative menus and specialty items.

Tips for Success:

- Research and comply with local regulations and health codes.
- Choose a unique food concept that stands out from competitors.
- Use social media to announce your location and build a loyal customer base.

Food trucks are particularly successful in urban areas or during events where foot traffic is high.

2.6.3 Catering Services

Catering is a profitable side hustle for those who enjoy cooking for larger groups and special occasions like weddings, parties, and corporate events. It requires a keen eye for presentation and the ability to handle multiple orders simultaneously.

Advantages:

- High earning potential for large-scale events.
- Opportunities to build long-term relationships with repeat clients.
- Flexibility to specialize in a niche, such as vegan, ethnic, or gourmet cuisine.

Tips for Success:

- Invest in high-quality cooking equipment and serving ware.
- Offer customizable menus to cater to diverse customer needs.
- Partner with event planners or venues to expand your client base.

Catering can start as a home-based business and scale up as demand grows.

2.6.4 Bake Sale/Selling Homemade Goods

Baking and selling homemade goods is an excellent way to combine creativity with earning potential. Products like cakes, cookies, bread, and pastries are always in demand for celebrations and daily consumption.

Advantages:

- Affordable startup costs with the ability to work from home.
- Opportunities to cater to niche markets, such as gluten-free or organic baked goods.
- Creative freedom to design custom products for clients.

Tips for Success:

- Focus on presentation and packaging to attract customers.
- Use social media to showcase your baked goods and take orders.
- Collaborate with local cafes or farmers' markets for wider exposure.

Starting small with pre-orders or pop-up sales can help you test the market before expanding.

2.6.5 Creative Ventures Side Hustles

For those with artistic or creative talents, turning hobbies into a business can be both fulfilling and financially rewarding. Creative ventures allow individuals to share their passions while offering valuable services.

3.1 Selling Crafts at Local Markets

Handmade crafts, such as jewelry, candles, artwork, and textiles, are popular items at local markets and fairs. Selling your creations allows you to connect directly with customers who appreciate unique, handcrafted goods.

Advantages:

- Low-cost entry with the potential for high profit margins.
- Opportunity to showcase your creativity and craftsmanship.
- Direct interaction with customers to build brand loyalty.

Tips for Success:

- Research popular craft trends and incorporate them into your designs.
- Invest in a visually appealing booth or display to attract customers.
- Promote your market appearances on social media to drive foot traffic.

Selling crafts can also be complemented by an online store to reach a wider audience.

3.2 Music Lessons/Teaching Art

If you're skilled in music or visual arts, teaching others can be a rewarding and profitable side hustle. This can include piano lessons, guitar tutorials, painting workshops, or photography classes.

Advantages:

- Flexible schedule that accommodates both you and your students.
- Ability to work with students of all ages and skill levels.
- Potential to offer online lessons for greater accessibility.

Tips for Success:

- Create structured lesson plans tailored to individual needs.
- Advertise your services in local communities, schools, or online platforms.
- Build a strong reputation through word-of-mouth referrals and testimonials.

Teaching is not only a great way to earn but also an opportunity to inspire others and share your passion.

3.3 Photography/Videography Services

Photography and videography services are in demand for various occasions, including weddings, family portraits, business events, and marketing campaigns. This side hustle is perfect for individuals with technical skills and a creative eye.

Advantages:

- High earning potential for specialized photography, such as wedding or commercial shoots.
- Opportunities to work on diverse projects, keeping the work engaging.
- Ability to monetize your portfolio by selling stock photos or videos.

Tips for Success:

- Invest in quality equipment and editing software to deliver professional results.
- Build a portfolio showcasing your best work to attract clients.
- Offer packages or bundled services to cater to different budgets.

As your reputation grows, photography and videography can become a full-time business with consistent demand.

4. Creative Ventures: Where Passion Meets Profit

The realm of creative ventures provides a unique platform for individuals to transform their passions into profitable endeavors. From the artistry of handmade crafts to the intellectual pursuit of teaching and the captivating world of visual storytelling, these avenues offer a blend of creative expression and financial reward.

5. Selling crafts at local markets

Selling handcrafted goods at local markets provides a tangible connection between the creator and the consumer. Whether it's the intricate artistry of jewelry making, the rustic charm of pottery, or the vibrant hues of hand-painted textiles, these markets offer a platform to showcase unique creations and engage with a diverse clientele. Building a strong online presence through social media and cultivating a loyal customer base are essential for long-term success.

6. Music lessons/teaching art

For those with a deep passion for music or art, teaching offers a rewarding opportunity to share their knowledge and inspire the next generation of artists. Whether it's imparting the fundamentals of piano, guiding aspiring painters, or nurturing young dancers, teaching provides a fulfilling and intellectually stimulating experience. Building a strong reputation as a dedicated and effective instructor is crucial for attracting and retaining students.

7. Photography/videography services

The world of photography and videography offers a captivating blend of artistic expression and technical skill. From capturing the magic of weddings and the vibrancy of events to documenting the beauty of the natural world, these creative pursuits provide a unique perspective and a valuable service. Building a strong portfolio, developing a distinct creative style, and effectively marketing your services are essential for success in this competitive field.

In conclusion, the world of food and beverage and creative ventures offers a diverse array of opportunities for those seeking to transform their passions into profitable pursuits. By carefully considering their skills, interests, and the unique demands of each endeavor, individuals can embark on a rewarding journey of entrepreneurial exploration, turning their dreams into a reality.

Chapter 3: Leveraging Your Skills & Interests

To succeed in any venture, understanding your unique skills and passions is essential. When you leverage what you are naturally good at and combine it with what you love, you not only enjoy the process but also create opportunities for sustainable success. This chapter explores practical ways to identify your skills and passions, laying the foundation for building a fulfilling and profitable side hustle.

1. Identifying Your Unique Skills and Passions

Identifying your skills and passions involves self-reflection and exploration. Skills are the abilities you've acquired through experience, education, or training, while passions are the activities or topics you are deeply enthusiastic about. The intersection of these two elements forms the basis of a successful and enjoyable pursuit.

1.1 Skills Assessment

A skills assessment helps you recognize your strengths, talents, and areas of expertise. These can include technical, creative, interpersonal, or organizational skills.

Steps to Assess Your Skills:

1. **Make a Skills Inventory**:

   - List all the skills you've gained from your job, education, or hobbies.
   - Include both hard skills (e.g., programming, graphic design) and soft skills (e.g., communication, leadership).

2. **Ask for Feedback**:

   - Seek input from colleagues, friends, or mentors to gain an outside perspective on your strengths.
   - Ask them what they think you excel at or what they've seen you succeed in.

3. **Reflect on Past Achievements**:

   - Review projects or tasks you've completed successfully.
   - Identify what skills you used and how they contributed to your success.

4. **Take Online Skills Tests**:

   - Use free tools or platforms to evaluate your abilities in areas like problem-solving, creativity, or technical expertise.

Examples of Skills You Might Identify:

- Writing and editing
- Photography or videography
- Financial planning
- Event organization
- Social media management

1.2 Interest Inventories

Interest inventories are tools that help you uncover what you truly enjoy. Unlike skills, which are learned, interests are natural inclinations or activities that bring you joy and fulfillment.

How to Discover Your Interests:

1. **Reflect on Your Free Time:**

   - What activities do you enjoy during your downtime?
   - Consider hobbies, books you like to read, or topics you research out of curiosity.

2. **Think About Childhood Interests:**

   - Recall activities you loved as a child. Often, childhood passions resurface as adult interests.

3. **Analyze What Energizes You:**

   - What tasks or conversations leave you feeling excited and motivated?
   - Consider areas where you lose track of time because you're so immersed.

4. **Use Interest Assessment Tools:**

   - Explore online resources or career counseling tools like the Holland Code or Strong Interest Inventory to pinpoint your interests.

Examples of Interests:

- Arts and crafts
- Fitness and wellness
- Technology and innovation
- Gardening or nature exploration
- Travel and cultural experiences

1.3 Brainstorming Sessions

Brainstorming is a creative process that helps you connect your skills and passions to potential opportunities. This step involves exploring all possible ways to use your abilities and interests productively.

Steps to Brainstorm Effectively:

1. **Combine Skills and Interests:**

   - Look for overlaps between your skills and passions. For instance, if you're good at writing and love fitness, consider writing fitness blogs or creating workout guides.

2. **List Potential Opportunities:**

   - Write down all the possible ways to monetize your skills and interests without judging their feasibility initially.

3. **Identify Gaps in the Market:**

   - Research existing businesses or services in your area of interest and find gaps you could fill.

4. **Seek Inspiration:**

   - Talk to people in your network, read success stories, or explore online communities for ideas on turning your skills and passions into income streams.

Brainstorming Example:

- **Skill:** Cooking
- **Interest:** Health and wellness
- **Opportunity:** Offer meal prep services focused on healthy, balanced meals or host cooking classes.

Notes. Leveraging your skills and interests is a powerful way to align your personal strengths with your professional goals. Through a thorough skills assessment, interest inventory, and brainstorming sessions, you can discover unique opportunities that bring value to others and fulfillment to yourself. By understanding what you're good at and what excites you, you can create a meaningful and rewarding path that sets the stage for success.

Turning your hobbies into an income-generating activity is one of the most fulfilling ways to earn money. It allows you to do what you love while creating value for others. Whether it's cooking, photography, crafting, or fitness, almost any hobby can be monetized with the right strategy and dedication. This chapter explores how to transform your passion into profit and provides practical steps to find your niche.

Turning Hobbies into Income

The first step in monetizing your hobby is recognizing its potential as a business opportunity. Hobbies you're passionate about often come with skills or knowledge that others may be willing to pay for.

Examples of Monetizing Hobbies

1.1 Turning a Love for Cooking into a Meal Prep Service
If you enjoy cooking and are skilled at meal planning, you can offer a meal prep service. This involves preparing healthy, ready-to-eat meals for busy individuals or families.

Steps to Start:

- Identify a target audience (e.g., working professionals, fitness enthusiasts, or individuals with dietary restrictions).
- Develop a range of menu options that cater to different preferences and needs.
- Focus on packaging and presentation to make your meals appealing.
- Use social media or local advertising to promote your services.

Meal prep services are particularly appealing in urban areas where people seek convenience without compromising on nutrition.

1.2 Turning a Passion for Photography into a Wedding Photography Business
If photography is your passion, consider specializing in wedding photography. Weddings are significant events, and couples are willing to invest in capturing their memories professionally.

Steps to Start:

- Build a portfolio by photographing events for friends, family, or community gatherings.
- Invest in high-quality camera equipment and editing software.
- Market your services on platforms like Instagram, Pinterest, and wedding directories.
- Offer packages that include pre-wedding shoots, event coverage, and post-production.

Wedding photography can be a lucrative niche, especially if you develop a reputation for delivering exceptional results.

1.3 Other Examples

- **Crafting**: Turn handmade crafts into an Etsy shop or sell at local markets.
- **Fitness**: Offer personal training sessions or online fitness coaching.
- **Gardening**: Sell plants, offer landscaping services, or teach gardening workshops.
- **Writing**: Publish eBooks, write blogs, or offer freelance writing services.

2. Finding Your Niche

Identifying a niche is crucial for standing out in a competitive market. A niche is a specific area of expertise within your chosen field that allows you to cater to a targeted audience. By narrowing your focus, you can become an expert in your niche and build a loyal customer base.

Steps to Find Your Niche

2.1 Identify Your Strengths and Interests
Start by listing your hobbies, skills, and interests. What do you enjoy doing? What are you naturally good at? For example:

- Are you a skilled baker? Consider creating custom cakes or niche desserts.
- Do you have a knack for fitness? Focus on a specific type of training, such as yoga or weightlifting.

2.2 Research Market Demand
Assess whether there's a demand for your hobby in the market. Research trends, customer needs, and competitors. Use tools like Google Trends, social media, and online forums to understand what people are looking for.

Questions to Consider:

- Are people willing to pay for the service or product you're offering?
- Is the market already saturated, or is there room for a fresh approach?
- What unique value can you bring to your audience?

For example, if you're passionate about photography, you could specialize in a niche like maternity photoshoots or pet photography.

2.3 Understand Your Target Audience
Once you've identified a niche, define your target audience. Who are they? What are their needs and pain points? For instance:

- A meal prep service might target health-conscious professionals.
- A photography business could focus on young couples planning weddings.

Tailoring your services to a specific group helps build stronger connections and increases your chances of success.

2.4 Test and Refine Your Idea

Before fully committing, test your niche idea on a small scale. For example:

- Offer your services to a few clients at a discounted rate.
- Sell a limited batch of products to gauge interest and gather feedback.

Use the insights you gain to refine your offerings and ensure they meet customer expectations.

Tips for Niche Success

- **Be Unique**: Differentiate yourself by offering something others don't, whether it's a unique product, exceptional service, or a fresh perspective.
- **Stay Focused**: Avoid trying to appeal to everyone. A well-defined niche allows you to master your craft and cater effectively to your audience.
- **Adapt to Feedback**: Listen to your customers and continuously improve your offerings based on their input.

Notes. Turning your hobbies into income is an empowering way to achieve financial independence while doing what you love. By finding a niche and understanding your target audience, you can transform your passion into a sustainable and fulfilling business. The key is to combine creativity, dedication, and a strategic approach to create a unique offering that resonates with customers. With patience and persistence, your hobby can become not just a side hustle but a thriving venture.

Chapter 4: Building Your Side Hustle

Building a successful side hustle requires careful planning and a clear roadmap to guide your efforts. A solid foundation not only increases your chances of success but also ensures your venture is sustainable. This chapter focuses on creating a business plan, including key components like identifying your target audience, developing a marketing strategy, setting pricing, and creating a budget.

1. Creating a Business Plan

A business plan is a blueprint that outlines your goals, strategies, and the steps needed to achieve them. It provides clarity on how to structure your side hustle and serves as a guide for decision-making. Below are the essential components of an effective business plan.

1.1 Identifying Your Target Audience

Your target audience consists of the specific group of people who are most likely to purchase your product or service. Understanding their needs and preferences helps you tailor your offerings to meet their expectations.

Steps to Identify Your Target Audience:

1. **Define Demographics:**

   - Age, gender, location, income level, education, and occupation.
   - For example, a fitness coach might target health-conscious professionals aged 25–40.

2. **Understand Psychographics:**

   - Consider interests, values, and lifestyle choices.
   - A meal prep service may focus on individuals who value convenience and healthy eating.

3. **Analyze Problems and Needs:**

   - Identify the challenges your audience faces and how your side hustle can solve them.
   - Example: A wedding photographer addresses the need for high-quality, memorable event photos.

4. **Conduct Market Research:**

   - Use surveys, social media polls, and online forums to gather insights.
   - Study competitors to see who they're targeting and how you can differentiate yourself.

Target Audience Example:
A handmade jewelry business might target young adults (18–30) who appreciate unique, eco-friendly accessories.

1.2 Developing a Marketing Strategy

A marketing strategy outlines how you'll promote your side hustle and reach your target audience. Effective marketing helps you build brand awareness and attract customers.

Key Elements of a Marketing Strategy:

1. **Build Your Brand Identity:**

    - Create a unique brand name, logo, and tagline that reflect your business values.
    - Ensure consistency across all platforms, from social media to packaging.

2. **Choose the Right Marketing Channels:**

    - Use platforms where your target audience spends their time.
    - Example: Leverage Instagram for visually appealing products like crafts or food, and LinkedIn for professional services like consulting or coaching.

3. **Create Engaging Content:**

    - Post high-quality photos, videos, or blogs showcasing your product or service.
    - Share testimonials, behind-the-scenes content, or tips related to your niche to build trust.

4. **Leverage Word of Mouth:**

    - Encourage satisfied customers to recommend your services.
    - Offer referral discounts or incentives to loyal clients.

5. **Run Promotions:**

    - Launch limited-time offers, discounts, or giveaways to attract new customers and retain existing ones.

Example: A freelance graphic designer might use LinkedIn to share portfolio samples, client success stories, and design tips to attract professional clients.

1.3 Setting Pricing

Pricing your product or service correctly is crucial to attract customers and ensure profitability. Your prices should reflect the value you provide while staying competitive.

Steps to Set Pricing:

1. **Understand Your Costs:**

    - Calculate all expenses, including materials, time, tools, and overhead costs.
    - For example, a baker should account for ingredients, packaging, and electricity.

2. **Research Market Rates:**

   - Analyze competitors' pricing for similar products or services.
   - Position yourself competitively by offering unique value or competitive rates.

3. **Consider Your Value Proposition:**

   - Highlight what makes your offering unique (e.g., premium quality, eco-friendliness).
   - Customers are often willing to pay more for added value or personalized service.

4. **Test and Adjust:**

   - Start with an introductory price and gauge customer response.
   - Adjust based on demand, feedback, and profit margins.

Example: A freelance writer might charge $50 per blog post initially, increasing the rate as they gain experience and a portfolio.

1.4 Creating a Budget

A budget helps you manage your finances effectively by tracking income and expenses. It ensures your side hustle remains profitable and sustainable.

Steps to Create a Budget:

1. **List Startup Costs:**

   - Include initial investments like equipment, website hosting, or marketing materials.
   - Example: A photographer might budget for a camera, lenses, editing software, and portfolio website.

2. **Estimate Monthly Expenses:**

   - Track recurring costs such as supplies, subscriptions, or transportation.
   - Example: A food delivery side hustle may incur fuel and packaging costs.

3. **Project Your Income:**

   - Set realistic revenue goals based on your pricing and estimated sales.
   - Example: A tutor charging $20 per hour and working 10 hours a week can expect $800 monthly revenue.

4. **Monitor and Adjust:**

  - Regularly review your budget to ensure expenses don't exceed income.
  - Identify areas to cut costs or invest more for growth.

Budget Example:

Category	Estimated Cost
Startup Costs (camera, website)	$1,500
Monthly Expenses (marketing, tools)	$200
Projected Income	$2,000
Net Profit	$1,800

Notes. Building your side hustle begins with a well-thought-out business plan. By identifying your target audience, developing a marketing strategy, setting competitive pricing, and creating a detailed budget, you lay the groundwork for a successful venture. A structured approach ensures that your side hustle not only meets customer needs but also achieves financial sustainability, enabling you to grow and thrive over time.

Marketing & Sales: Driving Growth for Your Side Hustle

Marketing and sales are the lifeblood of any successful side hustle. Even the best products or services need effective promotion to attract customers and drive revenue. This section explores key strategies to market your side hustle, build strong relationships, and create a thriving business.

1. Social Media Marketing

Social media marketing is one of the most cost-effective and impactful ways to promote your side hustle. Platforms like Instagram, Facebook, TikTok, LinkedIn, and Twitter allow you to reach a large audience, showcase your offerings, and engage with potential customers.

Steps to Use social media Effectively:

1. **Choose the Right Platforms:**

  - ✓ Select platforms that align with your target audience.
  - ✓ Example: Use Instagram for visually appealing products like crafts or food, LinkedIn for professional services, and TikTok for entertaining, short-form content.

2. **Create High-Quality Content:**

- ✓ Share engaging posts, such as tutorials, behind-the-scenes videos, and customer testimonials.
- ✓ Use professional visuals and consistent branding to establish credibility.

3. **Engage with Your Audience:**

- ✓ Respond promptly to comments, messages, and inquiries.
- ✓ Interact with followers through polls, Q&A sessions, and live videos to build relationships.

4. **Use Paid Advertising:**

- ✓ Leverage targeted ads to reach specific demographics and boost visibility.
- ✓ Platforms like Facebook and Instagram allow you to set budgets and target based on location, age, interests, and more.

Example: A baker might share photos of their creations, post baking tips, and run promotions like "10% off your first order" to attract new customers.

2. Networking

Networking is an invaluable tool for growing your side hustle. Building connections with people in your industry or local community can open doors to opportunities, partnerships, and referrals.

Tips for Effective Networking:

1. **Attend Industry Events:**

- Participate in workshops, trade shows, or local meetups related to your niche.
- Bring business cards or flyers to share your contact information.

2. **Join Online Communities:**

- Engage in Facebook groups, LinkedIn forums, or Reddit threads where your target audience or peers gather.
- Share your expertise by answering questions or providing valuable insights.

3. **Leverage Existing Relationships:**

- Inform friends, family, and colleagues about your side hustle.
- Encourage them to spread the word to their networks.

4. **Collaborate with Others:**

- Partner with complementary businesses to reach new audiences.
- Example: A photographer could collaborate with a wedding planner to offer bundled services.

Example: A freelance web developer might join local business networking groups to meet small business owners who need websites.

3. Customer Service

Providing exceptional customer service is key to building trust, retaining customers, and encouraging word-of-mouth referrals. Satisfied customers are more likely to become repeat buyers and recommend your business to others.

Best Practices for Customer Service:

1. **Be Responsive:**

- Reply promptly to inquiries, messages, and complaints.
- Use email, chat, or social media to stay accessible.

2. **Exceed Expectations:**

- Go the extra mile to surprise and delight your customers.
- Example: Include a handwritten thank-you note or a small freebie with purchases.

3. **Handle Complaints Gracefully:**

- Listen to customer concerns without being defensive.
- Offer solutions, such as refunds, exchanges, or discounts, to resolve issues.

4. **Follow Up:**

- Check in with customers after a purchase to ensure satisfaction.
- Encourage them to leave reviews or provide feedback.

Example: An online tutor who provides personalized progress reports and additional resources earns loyalty by showing genuine care for students' success.

4. Building a Strong Online Presence

A strong online presence establishes credibility and makes it easier for customers to find and trust your business. From a professional website to active social media profiles, your online presence is often the first impression potential customers have of your side hustle.

Steps to Build Your Online Presence:

1. **Create a Professional Website:**

    - Include essential information like services/products, pricing, contact details, and testimonials.
    - Use user-friendly designs and ensure your site is mobile-responsive.

2. **Optimize for Search Engines (SEO):**

    - Use relevant keywords in your website content and blog posts to improve visibility in search engine results.
    - Example: A yoga instructor might use keywords like "beginner yoga classes" or "online yoga sessions."

3. **Leverage Online Directories:**

    - List your business on platforms like Google My Business, Yelp, or niche-specific directories.
    - Ensure your information is accurate and consistent across platforms.

4. **Encourage Online Reviews:**

    - Request satisfied customers to leave reviews on Google, Facebook, or your website.
    - Positive reviews build trust and attract new clients.

5. **Stay Active on Social Media:**

    - Post regularly, engage with followers, and share updates about your side hustle.
    - Use analytics tools to track performance and refine your strategy.

Example: A graphic designer might showcase their portfolio on a sleek website, share design tips on Instagram, and engage with other creatives on LinkedIn.

Notes. Marketing and sales are critical to the success of your side hustle. By using social media strategically, networking effectively, delivering excellent customer service, and building a strong online presence, you can attract and retain customers while growing your business. Remember, consistent effort and a customer-focused approach are key to long-term success in marketing and sales.

Legal & Financial Considerations

Establishing a strong legal and financial foundation for your side hustle is crucial for long-term success. Properly handling these aspects protects your business, ensures compliance with regulations, and keeps your finances organized. This section covers essential topics such as taxes, insurance, legal structure, and tracking income and expenses.

1. Taxes

Understanding and managing taxes is a critical responsibility for side hustle owners. Failure to comply with tax laws can result in penalties and legal issues.

Key Tax Considerations for Your Side Hustle:

1. **Register Your Business (If Required):**

   - Determine if your side hustle needs to be registered with local tax authorities.
   - Obtain any required tax identification numbers or licenses.

2. **Understand Tax Obligations:**

   - Report your side hustle income, even if it's part-time or seasonal.
   - Learn which taxes apply, such as income tax, value-added tax (VAT), or self-employment tax.

3. **Track Deductions:**

   - Keep records of business expenses to reduce taxable income.
   - Common deductions include supplies, software, travel expenses, and home office costs.

4. **Set Aside Funds for Taxes:**

   - Save a portion of your earnings (e.g., 20-30%) to cover taxes.
   - Consider making quarterly estimated tax payments if required.

5. **Seek Professional Help:**

   - Consult a tax professional or accountant to ensure compliance and maximize deductions.
   - Use software like QuickBooks or Wave for easier tax preparation.

Example: A freelance writer can deduct expenses for a laptop, writing software, and internet service as part of their business costs.

2. Insurance

Insurance is essential for protecting your side hustle from unforeseen risks. Depending on your industry and location, different types of insurance may be necessary.

Types of Insurance to Consider:

1. **Liability Insurance:**

   - Covers damages or injuries caused by your products, services, or business activities.
   - Example: A photographer might need liability insurance in case of equipment damage at an event.

2. **Professional Liability Insurance (Errors & Omissions):**

   - Protects against claims of negligence or mistakes in your work.
   - Example: A consultant might need this coverage to guard against claims of inaccurate advice.

3. **Property Insurance:**

   - Covers equipment, tools, or inventory used in your side hustle.
   - Example: A food vendor may insure their cooking equipment against theft or damage.

4. **Health and Disability Insurance:**

   - Ensures financial protection if you are unable to work due to illness or injury.

5. **Home-Based Business Insurance:**

   - If you operate from home, ensure your home insurance policy covers business-related activities or get an add-on policy.

3. Legal Structure (Sole Proprietorship, LLC)

Choosing the right legal structure for your side hustle affects taxes, liability, and operational flexibility.

Common Legal Structures:

1. **Sole Proprietorship:**

   - Simple and low-cost to set up.
   - The owner and the business are legally the same entity, meaning personal assets can be at risk for business debts.
   - Suitable for small, low-risk ventures like freelancing or tutoring.

2. **Limited Liability Company (LLC):**

   - Separates personal and business assets, reducing personal liability.
   - Offers tax flexibility; income can be taxed as a sole proprietorship or corporation.
   - Ideal for side hustles with moderate to high risk or significant assets.

3. **Partnership:**

   - Shared ownership between two or more individuals.
   - Partners share profits, losses, and legal responsibilities.
   - Suitable for joint ventures like event planning or co-run businesses.

4. **Corporation:**

   - A more complex structure with legal and tax benefits.
   - Generally not necessary for most side hustles unless you plan significant growth.

Example: A graphic designer might start as a sole proprietor but transition to an LLC as their client base and revenue grow, ensuring personal asset protection.

4. Tracking Income and Expenses

Proper financial tracking is essential for managing your side hustle efficiently. It ensures you stay organized, plan for growth, and prepare for taxes.

Best Practices for Tracking Finances:

1. **Open a Separate Business Account:**

   - Keep business finances separate from personal accounts for easier tracking and accountability.

2. **Use Accounting Software:**

   - Platforms like QuickBooks, FreshBooks, or Wave simplify income and expense tracking.
   - Automate invoicing, expense categorization, and financial reporting.

3. **Maintain Detailed Records:**

   - Keep receipts, invoices, and transaction records organized and accessible.
   - Use digital tools or apps to scan and store documents.

4. **Monitor Cash Flow:**

   - Regularly review income versus expenses to ensure profitability.
   - Identify areas where you can cut costs or invest for growth.

5. **Hire a Professional:**

   - If managing finances becomes overwhelming, work with an accountant or bookkeeper to stay compliant and efficient.

Example: A craft seller on Etsy might track materials, shipping costs, and platform fees to calculate net profit accurately.

Notes. Addressing the legal and financial aspects of your side hustle is critical to its long-term success. By understanding your tax obligations, securing appropriate insurance, choosing the right legal structure, and keeping detailed financial records, you can protect your business and ensure smooth operations. Taking these steps not only minimizes risks but also provides peace of mind as you focus on growing your venture.

Chapter 5: Maintaining Motivation & Avoiding Burnout

Running a side hustle can be incredibly rewarding, but it also demands time, energy, and focus. Balancing your hustle with other responsibilities can lead to stress and burnout if not managed effectively. This chapter explores strategies to maintain motivation, manage time wisely, and stay resilient in the face of challenges, all while prioritizing self-care and support.

1. Setting Realistic Goals and Deadlines

Setting clear, achievable goals provides direction and keeps you motivated. Unrealistic goals, however, can lead to frustration and burnout.

How to Set Realistic Goals:

1. **Use the SMART Framework:**

    - ✓ **Specific:** Clearly define what you want to achieve.
    - ✓ **Measurable:** Quantify your progress with metrics.
    - ✓ **Achievable:** Ensure the goal is within your reach given your current resources.
    - ✓ **Relevant:** Align goals with your overall vision and priorities.
    - ✓ **Time-Bound:** Set a deadline to create urgency and accountability.

2. **Break Goals into Smaller Steps:**

    - Divide larger objectives into manageable tasks.
    - Example: If launching a website, start with choosing a domain name, then creating content, and finally designing the site.

3. **Prioritize Goals:**

    - Focus on tasks that will have the greatest impact.
    - Avoid overloading yourself with too many goals at once.

4. **Celebrate Milestones:**

    - Acknowledge your progress, no matter how small, to stay motivated.

Example: A tutor aiming to gain 10 new clients in three months can set weekly targets for outreach and marketing efforts.

2. Time Management Techniques

Efficient time management ensures you balance your side hustle with personal and professional commitments.

Effective Time Management Strategies:

1. **Use a Planner or Calendar:**

    - Schedule specific blocks of time for your side hustle.
    - Include deadlines and reminders to stay on track.

2. **Apply the 80/20 Rule (Pareto Principle):**

    - Focus on the 20% of activities that yield 80% of your results.
    - Example: A blogger might prioritize writing and promoting content over perfecting the website design.

3. **Practice Time Blocking:**

- Dedicate specific periods to tasks like brainstorming, marketing, or client meetings.
- Avoid multitasking to improve focus and efficiency.

4. **Set Boundaries:**

- Clearly define work hours to prevent your side hustle from encroaching on personal time.
- Learn to say no to non-essential tasks or opportunities.

3. Staying Organized and Productive

Organization is the backbone of productivity. A cluttered workspace or scattered approach can lead to wasted time and missed opportunities.

Tips for Staying Organized:

1. **Digitize Your Workflow:**

- Use tools like Trello, Asana, or Notion to manage tasks and track progress.
- Store important documents in cloud-based storage like Google Drive or Dropbox.

2. **Create a Daily To-Do List:**

- Start each day by outlining your priorities.
- Check off completed tasks to build momentum.

3. **Eliminate Distractions:**

- Identify and minimize interruptions, such as excessive phone use or noisy environments.
- Use apps like Focus@Will or Freedom to stay concentrated.

4. **Regularly Declutter:**

- Keep your physical and digital workspace tidy to avoid unnecessary stress.

Example: A craft seller could organize inventory by product category and track stock levels using a simple spreadsheet.

4. Dealing with Setbacks and Challenges

Setbacks are inevitable in any entrepreneurial journey, but how you respond determines your ability to persevere.

Strategies for Overcoming Challenges:

1. **Adopt a Growth Mindset:**

   - View setbacks as opportunities to learn and improve.
   - Reflect on what went wrong and adjust your approach accordingly.

2. **Stay Solution-Oriented:**

   - Focus on actionable steps to resolve issues rather than dwelling on the problem.

3. **Seek Feedback:**

   - Reach out to mentors, peers, or customers for constructive insights.

4. **Practice Resilience:**

   - Remind yourself of your long-term goals and successes to maintain perspective.

Example: If a catering service faces negative feedback, use it as an opportunity to refine recipes or improve customer communication.

5. Finding a Support System

Building a strong network of support helps you stay motivated and navigate challenges more effectively.

How to Build Your Support System:

1. **Connect with Like-Minded Individuals:**

   - Join groups or forums related to your niche.
   - Attend networking events or workshops to meet peers and mentors.

2. **Lean on Friends and Family:**

   - Share your goals and challenges with those closest to you.
   - Ask for emotional support or help with tasks when needed.

3. **Hire Help When Necessary:**

  - Outsource time-consuming tasks, like bookkeeping or social media management, to lighten your workload.

4. **Engage with Online Communities:**

  - Participate in Facebook groups, Reddit threads, or LinkedIn communities where entrepreneurs share advice and experiences.

6. Prioritizing Self-Care

Burnout is a real risk for side hustlers, but prioritizing self-care helps maintain your energy and enthusiasm.

Self-Care Tips:

1. **Schedule Breaks:**

  - Incorporate short breaks during work sessions to recharge.
  - Take full days off to reset and avoid overexertion.

2. **Focus on Health:**

  - Eat nutritious meals, stay hydrated, and get regular exercise.
  - Prioritize sleep to ensure optimal focus and decision-making.

3. **Practice Stress Management:**

  - Use relaxation techniques like meditation, yoga, or deep breathing.
  - Set aside time for hobbies or activities that bring you joy.

4. **Seek Professional Help if Needed:**

  - Consult a therapist or counselor if you feel overwhelmed or stressed.

Example: A freelance writer might start their day with a 10-minute meditation to set a positive tone and reduce anxiety.

Notes. Maintaining motivation and avoiding burnout requires a blend of clear goal-setting, effective time management, and self-care. By staying organized, tackling challenges with resilience, and surrounding yourself with a supportive network, you can achieve a healthy balance and sustain your passion for your side hustle. Remember, success isn't just about hard work—it's about working smart while taking care of yourself.

Conclusion:

Unleashing Your Entrepreneurial Spirit

This journey through the world of side hustles has unveiled a wealth of opportunities, from the flexibility of online marketplaces to the rewarding connections forged through local service ventures. We've explored the power of leveraging your unique skills and passions, transforming them into profitable ventures that align with your personal and financial goals.

Key Takeaways:

- **The Importance of Self-Reflection:** Understanding your skills, passions, and values is crucial for identifying side hustle opportunities that are both fulfilling and sustainable.
- **The Power of Community:** Building strong relationships with clients, customers, and other entrepreneurs can significantly impact your success.
- **The Value of Continuous Learning:** The world of side hustles is constantly evolving. Embrace continuous learning, adapt to new trends, and continuously refine your strategies.
- **The Importance of Persistence:** Building a successful side hustle requires dedication, perseverance, and the ability to overcome challenges.

Encouragement and Inspiration:

Remember, the path to entrepreneurial success is not always linear. There will be setbacks, challenges, and moments of doubt. But with perseverance, resilience, and a belief in your own abilities, you can overcome any obstacle. Embrace the journey, celebrate your accomplishments, and never stop learning and growing.

Call to Action:

Now is the time to take the first step. Identify a side hustle idea that excites you, create a plan, and take action. Start small, experiment, and learn from your experiences. Embrace the spirit of entrepreneurship, and discover the freedom and fulfillment that comes with building a life on your own terms.

Resources:

- **Online Marketplaces:** Fiverr, Upwork, Etsy, Amazon
- **Freelancing Platforms:** ProBlogger, MediaBistro, Freelancewriting
- **Business Planning Tools:** SCORE, Small Business Administration (SBA)
- **Financial Resources:** NerdWallet, Mint, Personal Capital
- **Community Resources:** Local chambers of commerce, small business development centers, co-working spaces

Frequently Asked Questions

What are the easiest side hustles to start?

Among the easiest side hustles to begin are those that require minimal upfront investment and offer flexibility. Online surveys and microtasks, for instance, can be completed in short bursts of time, making them ideal for those with busy schedules. Food delivery and ridesharing services also offer flexible schedules and relatively easy on-boarding processes, making them accessible to many. Pet sitting and dog walking can be particularly rewarding for animal lovers and often involve working within one's local community.

What are some side hustles that require little to no investment?

Several side hustles can be launched with minimal financial outlay. Online surveys and microtasks are often free to join, requiring only a computer or smartphone and an internet connection. Freelance writing, particularly for those with existing writing skills, may require minimal investment in software or tools. Similarly, social media management can be started with little to no investment if one possesses the necessary social media skills.

What are some high-paying side hustle ideas?

While income potential varies greatly, certain side hustles tend to offer higher earning potential. Experienced freelance writers and editors can often command premium rates for their services. Web development and design, due to the high demand for skilled professionals, can also be lucrative. Online tutoring and teaching, especially for specialized subjects, can also command higher rates.

How can I find clients for my side hustle?

Securing clients is crucial for any successful side hustle. Online platforms like Upwork, Fiverr, and Freelancer can connect freelancers with potential clients seeking their services. Networking at industry events, connecting with people within one's network, and building strong relationships can also lead to valuable client connections. Social media platforms can be leveraged to showcase skills and attract potential clients. For those offering local services, utilizing community boards, flyers, and word-of-mouth referrals can be effective strategies.

How can I balance my side hustle with my full-time job?

Balancing a full-time job with a side hustle requires effective time management and prioritization. Creating a schedule and adhering to it can help ensure that both commitments are met. Setting clear boundaries between work and personal time is essential to avoid burnout. Utilizing downtime, such as commutes, can be a productive way to work on side hustle tasks. If possible, outsourcing certain tasks can free up time and reduce the workload.

20 Untapped Income Streams 2025   By Wasike Cornelius

What are some important legal and tax considerations for side hustles?

Understanding the legal and tax implications of a side hustle is crucial. It is important to report any income earned from a side hustle to the appropriate tax authorities. Depending on the nature of the side hustle, obtaining necessary licenses and permits may be required. Additionally, considering insurance coverage for potential liabilities associated with the side hustle is important.

How can I increase my income from my side hustle?

There are several strategies to increase income from a side hustle. As experience and a strong reputation are gained, increasing rates for services can be a viable option. Expanding the range of services offered to existing clients or exploring new service offerings can also increase revenue streams. Enhancing marketing efforts to reach a wider audience and building a strong online presence through a professional website or portfolio can attract more clients.

What are some resources available to help me get started with a side hustle?

Numerous resources are available to support those interested in starting a side hustle. Online platforms like Udemy, Coursera, and Skillshare offer a wealth of courses on various side hustle topics. Books and articles provide valuable guidance on starting and growing a side hustle. Seeking mentorship or coaching from experienced entrepreneurs or business coaches can provide valuable insights and support. Local business organizations often offer resources and networking opportunities for aspiring entrepreneurs.

What if I don't have any special skills or experience?

Lack of specific skills or experience should not deter someone from pursuing a side hustle. Starting with entry-level options like online surveys or food delivery can provide a low-pressure way to gain experience. Developing new skills through online courses or workshops can open up new opportunities. Volunteering in a field of interest can provide valuable experience and connections.

Is it worth pursuing a side hustle?

Pursuing a side hustle can offer numerous benefits. Financially, it can provide extra income, contribute to debt reduction, or help save for future goals. Personally, it can foster personal growth by developing new skills and gaining valuable experience. Additionally, it can provide greater flexibility and independence compared to traditional employment